# UNTITLED

KT

---

Softcover ISBN: 979-8-9890630-2-4
E-book

---

Printed in the United States of America

---

Requests for information and for bulk orders should be addressed to:
KDT Global Consulting

www.kdtglobalconsulting.com
ktyler@kdtglobalconsulting.com

Special Quantity Available Upon Request

To Place an Order Contact:
KDT Global Consulting
www.kdtglobalconsulting.com
ktyler@kdtglobalconsulting.com

UPWARD
FORWARD
ONWARD
PRESS

Hey, my name is KT. I am a 17-year-old multi-talented writer, chef, musical artist, and basketball player. I was born in Chicago and later moved to Las Vegas. I love writing poetry and short stories to help me express myself more and get my thoughts, feelings, and emotions out of my head. I have always struggled with my mental health, and writing helps me figure out who I am more. Look forward to seeing the name "KT" worldwide and in many books.

**TO CONTACT KT FOR SPEAKING ENGAGEMENTS:**

letstalkaboutit.kt@gmail.com

# UNTITLED.1

There's so much we don't know.
I wonder all I know
And all I wish I knew, too.
Because the things I didn't know
Never affected me
Until I knew I didn't know them
And when I did know,
I wish I didn't
And then it was a constant cycle
Of knowledge's thirst, and ignorance's hunger.

# UNTITLED.2

My tears
Effortlessly
Collapse
As they attempt to grasp
An understanding of their release.
My realizations
Have pushed me to
That I am needy,
That I am weak,
And although these writings are my passion,
I am robbing myself through this poetry.
I may never
Piece this heart together
By reframing
From releasing
The areas of my life which hold zero peace.
I write this with a shattered soul
And broken mind,
Quick fingers
Doing circles around all this infinite time
I write when I should verbally express
The emotions that leave stains all over the place
That is too chaotic
That leaves everything a mess,
To set my soul free,
Is to be unfamiliar
With my being.
Therefore, I remain stuck
In who I am
As the opposite of what I must.

# UNTITLED.3

What is masculinity
If not the divulging interest in being the beast
That femininity could not control.
And what is femininity
If not, the leash
That masculinity is tamed on.

# UNTITLED.4

It was only once.
But that's the thing about addiction.
It only needs to be done once.
A blackout drunk can't casually drink.
A chronic smoker can't smoke socially.
You can't gently hurt yourself.
Clean for a few months, but the number is sullied.
I see it in every separated edge,
And a piece of cutlery I pass,
And especially on days like these
Where I'm not terribly depressed
But I still have to search for a purpose.
It's never easy.
Sometimes, I forget I was an addict.
Maybe you never truly heal from addiction.

# UNTITLED.5

Mysterious…
Why must everyone want to be mysterious?
Do they not want to be seen?
Heard,
Or even known?
Why would they want to sink into the background
Instead of being in the spotlight?
That is the mystery I will never understand

# UNTITLED.6

Poetry doesn't have a rhyme
It doesn't need to be long or short
It simply just needs to
Be able to touch and reach
The most isolated and darkest areas.
In our souls

# UNTITLED.7

The soul wants what the soul wants.
We have no control of
What our soul wants and needs.
We simply just have to deal with whatever our soul wants
And what they would make our vessel do
In order to get it.

# UNTITLED.8

The walls of my throat
Burning…
Itching…
Needing to unleash how I feel,
And all the rushing thoughts in my head.
I can't tell you verbally,
So, I pick up my pen
And write instead.

# UNTITLED.9

The beauty of the night
Is the beauty of
The unheard and unseen.
For in the night,
One is able to go
Unrecognizable,
And finally, feel heard and seen.
That's why
I'm frustrated
With the
Night.

# UNTITLED.10

The curse of being creative
It's a huge burden
That, for some reason
Everyone envies.
Being creative is something
You shouldn't idolize.
You should be terrified,
You should be mortified,
Always having the need
To get something off your chest,
Always having a thought
Etched and not engrained
Into your head.

# UNTITLED.11

Who am I?
What defines me, I mean me?
Do I act this way
Cause I'm a product of my environment,
Or is it cause I'm heaven-sent?
I understand why I am the way I am:
It's probably because I decided
To smoke way more than a gram
And give too much care
About what people think on the gram.
When I sit back
And start to think about who I truly am.
All I can do is sit back and
Just say,
Damn.

# UNTITLED.12 (FROM A FRIEND)

"I love to sleep.
But I'm not gonna lie.
I go too deep.
I don't want to live life,
But I'm not allowed
To end mine with a knife."
-Anonymous Friend

# UNTITLED.13

When he takes over,
I feel trapped.
Feels like I'm in a
Endless void,
Staring into nothingness,
Feeling nothing,
And wanting to be nothing.
-Anonymous Friend

# UNTITLED.14

The brightest angels fall,
As do the prettiest stars.
The moon and the sun fall each day,
And the phoenix falls into ash.
But our celestial friends teach us this:
There is beauty and grace in falling.
Don't let it scare you.
Fall and fall hard,
And from there, you will rise.

# UNTITLED.15

In middle school,
I would show up with a smile on my face
And burst into laughing in class each day.
I was loud and outgoing,
Happy and carefree.
But somewhere along the line, I lost it -
That freedom….
That innocence…
Sometimes, I picture my younger self.
And worry, he won't even recognize me.

# UNTITLED.16

Go on a bike ride,
Roll a spliff up,
Spark up,
And get high.
Go home, listen to some music,
As you get inspired to
Pick up the pen and write.

# UNTITLED.17

She says she wants to be loved by a poet
Till she realizes that we would rather
Express our feelings and emotions
To a piece of paper instead of her.
We hide behind our words
And the spaces between them.
Why would I talk to you
When a pen and paper is the only thing
That has been there for me
And always listened?
It's hard to trust humans,
But easy to trust
A pen and pad.

# UNTITLED.18

You can't fix me.
You can't repair the damage
That was already here -
The damage from my father,
Who was damaged by his father,
For he was never loved by his father.
I told you,
You can't mend my wounds.
I just needed you next to me
As I heal myself.
Once you realized
You couldn't restore me,
You tore out my stitches.
Stitch your fingers in my open wounds,
You shut off my oxygen tank,
You turned off the lights,
As you walked out of my hospital room.

# UNTITLED.19

You show me a man who lost everything,
And I'll show you a man who gave it all away.
Show me someone who lost the will to fight,
And I'll show you a man beaten into submission.
Show me somebody
Who just wants to live,
And I'll show you a man.
I'll show you a man who's dead inside.
Don't forget,
Not everything you see on the outside
Is it a reflection of what's inside.
We all wear a mask, after all...
It's just a matter of ... why.

# UNTITLED.20

Why
Why should death be something
Everyone has to fear?
Do we only live because we are all afraid of dying?
Does anything good ever come from living?
Where do we go?
What do we do?
What's the purpose?
What you make it?
How many times can you make up a purpose?
And watch it fade away before
There's just no reason to have a purpose
Anymore.

# UNTITLED.21

As I sit here alone
And start to drift away
While listening to music,
Finally fleeing reality
With this great escape.
Longing for a hug
Or a sweet embrace,
But this is my life,
And I guess it's
Okay.

# UNTITLED.22

And I guess I
Just want to feel loved.
I want someone
Who would be there for me.
I want someone
To hold my hand,
And hold me tight,
And say,
"I'm here for you."
I want to feel acknowledged.
I want
To feel belonging.
I want to
Keep living life like
I'm invisible.
Sometimes, I feel great
About myself.
Then I realize,
I am a
Total loser
Nobody really messes with me.
And
That's
Okay.

# UNTITLED.23

We accept the love we deserve.
We only witness certain types of love in our life,
And we tend to
Just be in an endless cycle.
Reciprocating what we have
Learned and seen.

# UNTITLED.24

I used to be a good kid
With big dreams,
Had all the potential in the world,
But started smoking that weed.
Unlocked his true talent,
His true dream.
Outside smoking weed,
Pour out his soul
One piece of fucking paper.
Went from going to the NBA
Imma get on the big stage
And scream,
"Forget Y'all… We Paid."

# UNTITLED.25

I often wonder how Aphrodite would appear
If she ever came to me.
She would have warm brown eyes
(Some would say like milk chocolate),
She would have dark, curly hair,
She would make everyone around her cheerful,
And she would make me stare at her
For hours,
Fascinated
And captivated
By the aura
Of her soul, spirit, and mind.

# UNTITLED. 26

I often tell myself
That I am happy.
I learned
That if I smile
Long enough,
The facade wanes
Until it feels like reality.
But on those nights
When desolation consumes me,
It all comes crashing down.
All the pain and hatred
That I did hide
I just reappear…
And just like that,
These desolate nights
Become infinitely lonelier.

# UNTITLED.27

And if you ever find yourself
Craving to talk to me once more,
Thumb hovered over my name,
A message half typed out,
Don't hesitate.
Do not wait
Another month,
Second or day.
If you ever find yourself
Coming back to me,
Know that I have been waiting
For you since the day you left.
I will
Always and forever
Be waiting long for you.

# UNTITLED.28

The pain
Did not make me
A better person.
It did not teach me
Not to take anything for granted.
It did not teach me a single thing,
Except to be afraid
To fall in love with someone.

# UNTITLED.29

Draw a monster…
Why is it a monster?
What makes it a monster?
Is this monstrosity?
Truly something
To fear,
Or
Is it truly beautiful?

# UNTITLED.30

I picked it up
Once again today,
After months of
Not touching it
And cleansing myself.
I finally touched it,
Held it nicely
Between my two fingers,
Knowing I, too, was going
To regret.
After I was finished,
I watched as the line changed colors
While I sigh in relief.

# UNTITLED.31

Why do I feel like this?
Why must I feel like my mind is shutting down
And my body is becoming tired?
Every day is an endless
And repeating cycle
That just won't break.
And that sadness,
That depression,
Always tend to kick in
Whenever I start
To actually feel happy.
Oxygen becomes harder to breathe,
While marijuana smoke becomes easier,
And food becomes harder to swallow.
Growing older changes you,
But in ways
Our parents didn't prepare us for.
"Don't be too quick to grow up," mom and dad said.
And now I get it.
All I can remember is telling my mom
How much I wanted to be older,
But I would now do anything
To go back to the old days
And partake in my old ways
Where problems weren't
A Thing.

# UNTITLED.32

"Mental Health Matters"
Until you start hurting loved ones
Cause it's the only way you can cry for help.

"Mental Health Matters"
Till it looks like I'm sitting on my ass
And not doing anything.

"Mental Health Matters"
Until that one hurtful action
You did when you were at your lowest point
It's used against you.

"Mental Health Matters"
Until you start failing classes
And skipping school.

"Mental Health Matters"
Until you start showing real and raw emotion
And let your "other you" out.

"Mental Health Matters"
Until the distractions can't even distract anymore

"Mental Health Matters"
Until I show signs of addiction.

"Mental Health Matters"
Until you stop taking showers as much
Or even stop brushing your teeth.

"Mental Health Matters"
Until you constantly trying to find someone to make you feel loved
Cause you can't love yourself.

"Mental Health Matters"
Until you actually try and ask for help.

"Mental Health Matters"
Till you're gone…. And Dead.

# UNTITLED.33

The most powerful institution in the world
Is your mind.
The real everyday battles
Take place there.
Once you change your mindset,
You can achieve anything.

# UNTITLED.34

Homicides
Run through my mind day and night.
I forgot how to cry.
It's hard to fight off these demons
Once they come inside.
Something ain't right.
So, I fill this blunt up,
Roll Up,
Spark Up,
And get high.
Why do I do this shit?
It's just to chill my mind.
I had to find something
That would heal the pain inside.

# UNTITLED.35

The scariest part about adulthood
To me is what happens when the depression hits.
I would still have to function
And get my shit together,
Without being able to physically function.
Get out of bed,
Take a shower,
Brush my teeth,
Or even eat.
Worst part -
I'll be living alone.

# UNTITLED.36

Numb is how I feel.
Nothing appeals
To me anymore.
Nothing takes
Me out of this mental feeling
Of blankness,
This feeling of a desire to cry or weep.
But when I try,
Nothing is coming out.
How do I empty this tear bucket,
Building up inside of me,
If my emotions won't even
Express the pain
That is overflowing
And living rent-free
In my head?

# UNTITLED.37

I used to get sad
Because I got cut,
But it's funny
Cause now I cut
Because I get sad.
I don't know what it is
About a sharp piece of metal
Gliding on my skin
That draws so much....
Attention,
Gratification,
And adrenaline to me.
But now, most of the time,
It's all I can think about:
Just one more sting,
One more slash,
One more cut,
And then I'll stop.
But then I have to continue,
Because once never felt enough.

# UNTITLED.38

Being alone and feeling alone are two different things.
I love being alone
But I hate feeling alone.
And I never felt more alone
Then I do right now.
I'm always checking my phone,
Looking for a new notification,
But there never is one.
I feel like there is no one to go to,
Or talk to,
Even though I have enough friends
And even loved ones.
But my mind loves to
Keep me isolated
In this lonely feeling
Of disbelief
That I will always
Feel like this,
And it will never end
Till it ends.

# UNTITLED.39

After just one relapse,
It just welcomes more -
More daily
That I cannot control
The urges anymore.
Everyone says relapsing is
A part of healing,
But how many times
Must I relapse
In order to
Feel healed?

# UNTITLED.40

If you asked me what's wrong,
I wouldn't be able to tell you
Cause to be honest,
I'm not really sure what's wrong with me.
It's just an overwhelming sadness
That consumes me,
That creeps in day by day.
And most of the time,
It isn't caused by anything.
It just makes me confused
And unsure about myself
Cause I don't really understand
Why I'm feeling
The way I do.

# UNTITLED.41

I tell myself to move on
Because I would rather cut off my hand
Then to ever reach for you again.
But I am a weak man
And a liar.
I know if you
Was to say the right words,
I will be at your door
With flowers,
A poem,
And a missing hand.

# UNTITLED.42

"What flavor should I get?"
"Are we getting ice cream?"
"Do you have a pencil sharpener?"
"What are we coloring?"
"Pass me a lighter."
"Whose birthday, is it?"

What an innocent child I wish I still was.

# UNTITLED.43

Hi, my name is KT,
And I'm from the murder capital.
I'm from if you get told, "Check it out,"
You don't go check it out.
I'm from a beautiful city
With ugly people.
Hot summer days outside,
Ruined, ending early -
All cause of a drive-by
And some niggas that love "being outside."
I'm from a place where if you got talent,
Get out quick, before you lie on the street dead.
I'm from a place where it's hella windy outside,
And we love to rep our city
Till we die.
Old church on the Corner,
Don't know how that store thrived.
Where grandmas are so scared,
They'd rather just stay inside.
I'm from a place that's just like the trenches;
We've got 15-year-olds with PTSD
And psychopathic tendencies.
Yeah, and that's where I'm from.
That's home.
And I wouldn't change
Not a damn thing.

# UNTITLED.44

The most beautiful souls
Are shaped by ugly experiences.
They were once sweet and innocent,
And even if they are still nice,
They have scars
With haunting background stories.
So be tender,
Kind,
And patient with these people.

# UNTITLED.45

I know love exists
Because I exist,
And I'm full of it.
So, even if everyone in the world
Doesn't have love,
There will always
Be at least one -
And that's me.

# UNTITLED.46

I was ashamed of myself
When I realized that
Life is a masquerade party,
And I attended with my face.
Everyone pretending,
Everyone one manipulating,
Deceiving people,
Deducing people,
Lying and lying -
Oh, all the lying,
Oh, all the lies.
And I decided to show up
As myself.
So naturally,
I become like them.
But you get mad at me when I do it
And call me a…
Monster.

# UNTITLED.47

And to feel is not to love,
To hope is not to love,
And to wish is not to love.
To love is to act.
It is to make the decision,
An active conscious voice,
At every waking moment,
To preserve your humanity,
To keep the world spinning
On that, every axis,
To bring uniqueness to life,
One never seen nor heard -
An expression so complex,
It has to be experienced
In order to truly understand.

# UNTITLED.48

Soberness feels freeing,
But addiction sparks hope.
And being hopeful
Is a stronger and more passionate emotion
Then feeling free.
That is why recovering is hard -
Because it's a constant inward conflict
Between being free
Or
Having hope.

# UNTITLED.49

The pieces of being unheard or unseen -
Those who are unheard or unseen go unnoticed.
There are no expectations,
There is no drama,
There is no anxiety.
They simply just exist
Without existing.

# UNTITLED.50

Mary gave birth to a son,
Not a God.
She knew his fate,
She knew this when he had growing pains
And loose teeth.
She knew this when he got runny noses
And dirt on his cheek.
What did he call her?
What was his favorite meal she cooked?
She held him as her son,
While the world will always see him as God.

# UNTITLED.51

Sometimes, I fall asleep
With the lights on.
Maybe it's because I'm lazy,
Don't want to get out of my bed,
Get out of my clothes,
Get into my head,
Which I do sometimes in the dark.
Maybe I fall asleep with the lights on
Because with them off, I trip
Over the mess that my life is.
Maybe sometimes I fall asleep with the lights on
Because I'm still waiting on you.
I want you to pass by
And see my light.
I want to wake up to the sound of you
Crinkling into the covers.
And I want you
To ask me whether or not
I want the lights on
Or off,
So, I can say,
"It doesn't matter."

# UNTITLED.52

Will I ever get better?
Will I ever be, okay?
They say I will if I try.
They say I will if I just face it.
But every time I do,
It only seems like it gets worse.
So, I ask again:
Will I ever get better?
Will I ever be, okay?

# UNTITLED.53

If you were in my head,
You'll be scared too...

If you saw what I think,
You'll be scared too...

If you saw what I fantasized over,
You'll be scared too...

Just live one day in my head.

And

You'll be scared too...

# UNTITLED.54

I wished I cried like a man,
Which is not at all.
MEN DON'T CRY.
I don't think
They've forgotten how it wasn't passed down,
Which is sad and it makes me cry.
I think if some men knew just how ugly they were,
Then, they would cry.
But they don't, so they don't.
To see tears in their eyes
Means they do not know,
And it's easier for boys…. men
To be ugly,
But
It's harder for them to cry about it.

# UNTITLED.55

Dear old me,
We're doing a little better now.
Seen our darker days
Switch to light,
And our problems, we finally figured them out.
I'm proud of us today
Cause
Even though we found it hard,
We still pushed back and carried on.
Dug our feet in once more,
And to the mirror said,
"We are not done."
Despite it all, we will still run,
Cause if we're alive and we're breathing,
Then we must be someone.
And now we wake up a little earlier,
Without the burning in mind.
I know you feel a burden right now,
But trust me, we'll learn it in time.
That there's patience with problems,
It takes some work to beat the fear.
So, take a pause and breath, kiddo cause
You're more than a year.
You're more than a moment.
So, know that it doesn't define you.
Just cause it's not happening right now
Doesn't mean there are heights you won't climb to.
So, try to live for today,
And live for tomorrow when it comes.
From you to yourself,
Yourself who is one.

# UNTITLED.56

Mom says people change,
But I still go quiet in a large group.
I still turn on my nightlight after a nightmare.
I still love wholeheartedly,
And I still pretend that I don't.
Dad says people don't change;
However, I think instead,
We simply grow.
Maybe the hard things remain hard,
But maybe by God's good grace,
Or a little bit of hard work,
We will learn to make a bed
Out of our discomfort.
(Or at least I hope.)

# UNTITLED.57

I discuss with my teacher
The theories of world change.
We are learning so much,
I thought.
I look around the room,
Imagining everyone must feel as I do,
Only to find they don't.
Though the people who care,
We always find it.

# UNTITLED.58

I outworked my ignorance
And developed such prudence
I could see the future in alluring color.
It was my brightest gift,
Yes, somehow, my darkest curse.
I never enjoyed anything beneath achievement,
And I knew that wasn't living,
But it was the only way
That I knew how to stay alive.

# UNTITLED.59

Staying in,
Awfully plain biscuits,
TV advertisements,
Waiting for the regular checkout,
Grocery list,
Letters,
Slow music,
Complete silence,
A collection of stamps,
Fancy literature,
Original citations,
Physical newspaper's
Talking about the younger generation
Like I'm not a part of it.

Old Soul.

# UNTITLED.60

Who will be the boogie man?
We gotta uproot the fear
Deify something,
Something that gives the people strength
So,
Who will be the boogie man?
Who will give the kids light?
Guarantee their future is bright?
What's done in the dark brings growth
So, who wants to be the seed?
Who wants to shake it like Django?
Strike justice through a colonizer's neck?
Staple them to a tree as a poster,
And ride through the black belt screaming,
"Who's next?"

# UNTITLED.61

You want to educate the black masses,
So, you up in Uni taking classes,
But what's a Negro education?
I…I mean Black.
But my question remains the same
Is your goal to assimilate,
Or teach people game?
Did you know they keep us poor?
So, we can buy into their ways?
We call each other broke,
Yet we all scrapping wage.
Crumbs to a cake
So, you can see through the veil?
Can you break down the intersectionality you, see?
If so do tell,
Educate the masses,
Show them how racism is institutionalized,
How they don't know themselves,
Cause they juggling two voices.
Makes you question
If either is even their own.

The American Dream
A black hole.

# UNTITLED.62

I'm strong for I have been weak.
I am wise for I have been foolish.
I am fearless for I have been afraid.
I am everything for I have been nothing.

# UNTITLED.63

20 years from now
You will be more disappointed by,
The things that you didn't do,
Than by the ones you did do.
So, throw off the bowlines,
Sail away from the safe harbor.
Catch the winds in your sails,
Explore…Dream…Discover!

# UNTITLED.64

We can easily forgive a child.
Who is afraid of the dark?
The real tragedy of life is
When adults are afraid of the light.

# UNTITLED.65

We are just suicidal kids
Talking each other out of committing
The sad irony of that.

# UNTITLED.66

What is black?
Is it joy,
The culture,
The pain?
What is black?
Can it outrun the rain?
Can shea butter really embrace the sun?
Or is it the pain
That is black?
To root for yourself,
Again, and Again
Digging into despair
And then repeat
Is black insanity?
Can a baby cradle a heart?
Can I pray that all mothers
See seeds become grapes
With an understanding of joy.

# UNTITLED.67

There are Kings of country
Kings of poor
Kings of rich
And Kings of bastards

I am King of none

The rejected
The abused
The neglected
The abandoned
And the unwanted

I am the King of None

I stand up for those
Who can't or those who
Are too scared too

I am the King of None

-KT


#2025loading

# NOTES

# NOTES

# NOTES

# NOTES

# N O T E S

Thank you, until next time!

Stay tuned to 2025

-KT

www.ingramcontent.com/pod-product-compliance
Lightning Source LLC
Chambersburg PA
CBHW070049040426
42331CB00034B/2768